Inspiration
THAT BRING
TRUE LIBERATION

Inspiration THAT BRING TRUE LIBERATION

Yvette A. Gayle

authorHOUSE®

AuthorHouse™
1663 Liberty Drive
Bloomington, IN 47403
www.authorhouse.com
Phone: 1-800-839-8640

Published by AuthorHouse   09/10/2012

ISBN: 978-1-4772-6627-4 (sc)
ISBN: 978-1-4772-6628-1 (e)

Library of Congress Control Number: 2012916265

CONTENTS

WRITTEN BY YVETTE GAYLE

Acknowledgement from the author

First and foremost, I want to thank almighty God for giving me the
Inspiration to initiate and to complete this inspirational book
I want to specially thank Clinton (Boobee) for his ongoing love,
Support, devotion, motivation and dedication
He played a significant role in the launching of this book
I want to thank Ansell for his encouragement
Additionally, I want to thank Jody, Tiffany, Pablo, Amsley,
Clover and my mother for believing in me
I pray that this book will be a blessing, and hope that it will captivate the
Hearts and mind of all who read it
May this book deliver comfort, insight, healing, inspiration
Deliverance and upliftment

RESIDENCE NOT A FACTOR

Whether you live in a luxurious big mansion bright and fair
Whether you live in a small single bamboo shack
Or in a little one room cottage located right by the road side in the country
I'll stay with you regardless of the circumstances
It doesn't matter where you choose to reside
Just as long as I am with you and we are together
If you happened to find yourself on top of the Mountain
Or way deep down in the valley
I'll be right there with you
To strengthen, to care and to comfort you
Love is the binding mechanism that holds us together
I'll come running to you even through

Your darkest day and throughout your darkest night
I want to be there to share in your triumphs
Your dilemmas and your victories
I want to offer support and bring
Good and wholesome things into your life
I want to maximize every moment shared with you

A SPECIAL KIND OF LOVE

Our love have grown passed Mount Everest
It has surpassed the deepest Ocean
And have crossed over the bluest Sea
Our love is never dull, but is ever renewed
With each passing moment, it's filled with passion
Flavored with never ending fragrance that lingers on and on
Our love is strong enough to conquer
Powerful enough to tear down any mountain
Sturdy enough to demolish the walls of defeat
With our love, there's nothing called failure
That word is simply not found in our vocabulary
Together we'll rise and embrace new horizons
Together we can conquer the world
Our love for each other will forever reign in our hearts
Undoubtedly, our love will never be
Shaken when tested, but will stand firm and secured

WISE INVESTMENTS

Whatever you put in, is what you'll get out
If you don't put in nothing, then you will not
Be able to get anything back in return
The best things in life is definitely not for free
Whatever you are trying to accomplish in life
Work hard at it, it doesn't matter if it's short or long term goals
Put in the time and effort, be persistent and committed
Stay on top of your game, stay focused
Don't procrastinate, stay motivated
Deposit into your life account smart and wise investments
When it's time to do the withdrawal from your account
You will enjoy the dividends and benefits
If for any unforeseen circumstances you get off track
Jump back on the band wagon, and continue striving
Be vigilant, sharpen your focus, be determined
Keep trying until you succeed and accomplish your goal

NEW LIFE

Life can be nice, it is like a bitter sweet journey
It's simply what you make of it
It is full of surprises, and disappointments
But can be very delightful
Each day is a gift, another opportunity to face life
Head on, with new desires, and new expectations
We got the power to navigate our life into the
Direction and way that we want it to go
Life becomes what you want it to be
You have the ability to dictate to it, and to tell it what you want
What you put into it, is what you'll get out of it
Even though things may look dismal at times
Be optimistic, look on the brighter side of life

SMALL BEGINNINGS

I wish that we all could learn to appreciate small beginnings
Because it's usually the starting point that leads to great success
It usually leads to better and even bigger things in life
Small beginnings are the first part of anything
Many successful people in life, usually climb the ladder
Of success by staring out very small
They climbed up little by little, and move up in stages
Some people struggled for many years
And never had the thought of giving up
Even when things didn't look so bright for them
They strived to keep their doors opened
Others took great financial risks
Amidst the challenges and hardships that they've endured
They did not give up when discouragement came
Today some of these same people are entrepreneurs
Running and maintaining their own business and making money
Don't despise small beginning
Thank God for small beginning

DREAM CHASER

Keep chasing your dreams, don't stop till
It materializes and become a reality
It's inevitable that oppositions and setbacks will come
But when they come, don't allow them to hinder your dreams
Don't let your guard down, persevere, and work hard
Continue to pursue your dreams, no matter what
Obstacles come, just keep fighting
Regardless of the circumstances
Don't walk away, never quit, or give up
Nothing in life comes easy
Be positive and confident about what you're trying to aspire
Be vigilant, be determined, continue to follow after your desire
Keep aiming high and soar like a mountain eagle
Do whatever it takes to achieve your goal

WIFE OF A TRUCKER

You're on the road again
Back on the road again
Because that is your job, your occupation
You're miles and miles away from me
When you've entered and exited every city, state and county
What a girl like me is supposed to do
I keep my cool, maintain my sanity
And pray the lord your soul to keep
My pillows are stained with teardrops as I cry myself to sleep
I visualize you in my dream and then it gets very deep
No one knows what I'm feeling, No one knows what I'm experiencing
Unless they're on the receiving end of the fence
What we have is special

What we have is magical and was done through divine connection
I never envisioned it would be you, you never envisioned it would be me
You've waited for me, I've waited for you
Together we embraced each other
Together we've embraced our destiny

RELAXATION TIME

Take the time out to unwind and to treat yourself
Indulge yourself into an evening of enjoyment and pure bliss
You worked so hard throughout the year
Let your hair down, take the time to relax
Put on your favorite red dress and slide into those new red pumps
Get out those matching earrings that you like
Put on your favorite jewelry
Grab your favorite Hors d' oeuvre or finger food
You could warm up some spicy buffalo wings
And get out your favorite dipping sauce
put out your favorite champagne
Put on some Mozart, Beethoven or Otis Redding
Light some nice scented candles, sit back and relax
And enjoy the ambience, you so richly deserve

THE MINDSET

I don't want to dwell on my past, It only hinder my future
By placing mental road block and set backs
I want to let go off the thoughts of *I should a or I could a*
I don't want to lament over what I don't have or what I didn't achieve
It's never too late to start
In order for me to move forward, I have to release the thoughts of yesterday
I want to hang it up and say goodbye to those
Negativity that ties me to my past
I am being more vigilant and persistent
I am not going to give up
I am going to embrace my dreams
The process is not going to be easy, but
I will continue to believe in myself
And will continue to take a stand
I'll embrace Today, I'll embrace now
I will let go off of yesterday
In order for me to move forward
And in order for me to increase productivity in my life

PUT YOUR HEART INTO IT

Whatever you choose to do in life
Do it to the best of your ability, it doesn't matter
How small or large the task
I've seen people doing your typical white collar job
Working in a factory making plastic bottles or working in a office
Others I've known they worked in fast food restaurants like Wendy's
McDonalds, Burger king, Wal-Mart, Kentucky Fried Chicken
The Dollar Store, just to name a few
They worked hard and put in long and tire some hours
Some received minimum wages for their hard work
But never complained, but remained committed
And just tried to make the ends meet
They were hardly late for work, they did not have a
Problem with tardiness, but tried to reach work on time
They didn't complained about their job responsibilities
But maintained a good mental and positive attitude
Some of these very same people became the manager or the
CEO of their company today
Put your heart into whatever you are doing
And be the very best that you can be

MAN OF MY DREAMS

You are like a delightful delicacy, no other man
Can be compared to you, you can never be matched or duplicated
You are unique and special, full of charm and charisma
You're so appetizing, I cannot get enough of you
It's difficult to curve this insatiable appetite that I have for you
With each passing moment, I am becoming more and more
Sentimentally attached, emotions are stirring deep inside of me
Every time I embrace thoughts of you
You're so warm and inviting
Since the day I met you until now
My heart is filled with joy and gladness
The aroma and scent that you give off is so tranquillizing
It leaves me wanting for more, you are so
Incredible gifted in everything that you do
Heaven must have sent you
Sweetheart, keep on smiling, keep on shining
Continue to deliver Aromatic Therapy

UNITY BECOMES STRENGTH

Isn't it a lovely thing when two hearts can meld
Beautifully in unison with the same aim and determination
Then the possibilities of achieving greatness becomes endless
There's no limitation to what you actually can achieve
When minds and hearts combine together
When there is no division, but only multiplication
Miracles do happen, and come alive
Unification can tear down any mountain or avalanches
It can definitely tear down a fortified city
Unity is strength, and can over take an army
Easily, efficiently, bravely and courageously
Without any intimidation, fear or defeat
So learn to develop a unification mentally
It will bring push you far beyond your wildest dreams

I AM NEVER GIVING UP

One more day in life's mystical journey
I'm standing firm and never giving up
Hurdle after hurdle, battle after battle
Triumph after triumph, victory after victory
I'm never putting down the baton
But will stay in the race
Many times I've gotten weak, and my feet buckled under
When the clouds and atmospheric turbulences of life
Got rough. I've learned to stay focused on my long term goals
I am staying strong and motivated
Because I have a dream, and an aim in view
I want to thank the ones who didn't
Stand with me or support me
You only motivated me to fight harder to succeed
And to reach my true potential in life
You pushed me further into my destiny
You allowed me to keep climbing the ladder of success

ONE VERY SPECIAL DAY

The intersection of our hearts just happened to
Cross paths one very special and marvelous day
We didn't meet by accident, it didn't happened by chance
Neither was it good luck, or by mere coincidence
This was in the making, and in the fire works for a very long time
It was all just a matter of time
Before the manifestation of two hearts
Would come together and become one
This plan was delicately and carefully orchestrated
By the one who's in charge of the universe, in charge of mankind
He rules supreme in the heavens, and he rule supreme on earth
He rules us, he rules our destiny
He rules in all the affairs of men
No one could ever figure out or ever phantom
The awesome work of our creator
He is always at work behind the scene

TRUE AND DELIGHTFUL LIBERATION

You have pulled me out of my closet
Yes, you have pulled me out of my shell
Just like how a caterpillar goes through
The process of metamorphosis, breaks
Out of it's skin, then develop into a butterfly
And takes on that beautiful colorful form
You have brought forth true liberation
You have allowed me spread my wings
And fly high like an eagle
You are my friend, you are my significant other
You are the catalyst for positive change
I want to take the time out to thank you
For all your support, and dedication
You have opened up a new chapter
And unfolded a new era in my life

THE ROSE

My one and only niece, I love you
Auntie admire the fine qualities and conduct
That you have displayed throughout the years
You are the perfect mold of what a niece should be
I am proud to be your aunt, so glad to have you in my life
Your smile matches your personality
The aura that you give off is so bright and fair
Those that surround you can feel the effect of it's residue
Those delightful light brown eyes are so beautiful
It brings about a special kind of glow
You are so fragile and dainty, just like a fresh scented pink rose

That the dew just fell off of
You are a gift sent from above
No wonder you're the only girl out of six wonderful nephews
You are so dignified and mature for such a young age
Your parents did a fine job with raising you

A TRUE FRIEND

A true friend is one who is in your life
Not only for a reason
But for a lifetime
Is one who understand your struggles
Your dilemmas, your weaknesses and failures
Is one that shares with you in your triumph and victories
That person should be supportive in every area of your life
A true friend should be honest
Open and willing to tell you the truth about yourself
Without being bias in any way
A true friend should embrace your dreams and aspirations
Should be willing to give concrete and constructive
Criticism whenever needed
Should be one who is able to shape
And inspire your life
With respect, honesty and integrity
These are the attributes of a true friend

HEART FELT PASSION

You are in my thoughts every minute of the day
What we share is special, it's magical, it's exciting
We were placed in each other's life for a reason
We were connected mystically by divine order
The feelings that I have towards you becomes uncontrollable at times
Sometimes, I attempt to harness the heart felt passion and desires
But it becomes difficult to retain
I have to let the feelings flow, and allow nature to take it's course
I have to be willing to embrace the fact
That love is a healthy and sweet part of life
There's no barrier to what the heart can conceive
My heart is like an endless reservoir that runs deep into a stream
It empties then refills itself and continue
Flowing back to you my love

NEGATIVITY PRODUCES UNPRODUCTIVITY

Some relationships are toxic, unhealthy and is just not good for us
Unhealthy relationships hinders growth. It will delay productivity
And will prevent you from moving effectively
It's hard to be around people who breathe negativity all the time
They speak doubt, lack faith, hope and motivation
How can such a person impact your life in a positive way
Sever unhealthy relationships and soul ties
They will place a damper on your life, and it will be
Hard for you to see your true potential,
Because their negativity keeps stifling you
Every time you take one step forward, their negativity
Allows you to take two steps backward
They are hindering you and preventing you from going forward
Toxic relationships set up barriers and road blocks
Get away so you can breathe easily and exhale properly

ONLY YOU

My darling you are simply the best
Time and time again, I've put you to the test
You undoubtedly are better than the rest
Your charm, charisma and fine appeal have
Mesmerized and have captured me
I am glad it's you and have no regrets
I cherish every moment spend with you
To be honest, no other man will do
I want to spend a lifetime of joy, peace and happiness with you
Just covered up and engulfed into our own little love nest
I just need to hear your voice, it tranquillizes and soothes my soul
I need to hear your voice because it's healing
Power warms and bring comfort to my inner being
I never want you to be far away from me
Even in my dream, I hear you calling out for me
In my vision I see you searching, diligently
And frantically until you found me
Together we are lost in our never ending love

ANGEL IN DISGUISE

You are the driving force behind my writings
Behind the inspirations, behind the whole apparatus
You have inspired me immensely in ways that you will
Never know or be able to understand
You have driven me and propelled me
Into a world of endless possibilities
You have allowed the dormancy of my writing abilities to come alive
You have opened up exciting doors and avenues
Allowing me to explore the hidden potential within myself
You've enabled me to develop new, fresh and modern ideas
In literature that are invigorating and surprising
You have allowed my world to come
Alive with creativity and vibrancy
You have helped me to give birth to my destiny

QUEEN MATERIAL

I've observed you from a distance for some time now
But never knew your true and hidden potential
As I got to know you better
I've noticed that you are reserved in your own way
Yet with sophistication and with elegance
You are unique, loaded with wisdom and full of diversity
In silence and deep meditation you've learned to
Renew your mind and regroup
As you execute a plan to take you throughout your day
You move cautiously with diligence and with careful planning
As you care for your family, and to those around you
You bring radiance to those who enters your path
Keep embracing life to the fullest
Continue to impart good and positive things into people's lives
You are a rose, so continue to bloom

MY BOOBEE

Boobee, my Darling, I shed a tear because of the happiness and joy
That you've brought into my life
Life is so uncertain, but one thing I'm certain about
And is that I love you now and for eternity
Just want to maximize each moment spend with you
Being with you makes the world a beautiful place to live
Your love has captured me, and held me captive
You have redefined my life in more ways than one
I'm devoted to your love because it's a special kind of love
More than the kind found in story books
More than Romeo and Juliet
I love you endlessly, and is devoted to our love
What I feel for you, I continue to bring out in my songs

WE ARE WHAT WE SPEAK

I believe that we become whatsoever we speak
Speak good and positive things into your life
Even though you don't see it the results right away
Continue to make and declare positive statements and affirmations
You are what you speak and believe
Speak good words into other people lives as well
Because some people have a poor self image
And speak negative things about themselves
Maybe you can help such a person to start viewing
Themselves in a positive way, your input might
Even help to build their self esteem
You can speak life or you can speak defeat
The power all lies within our tongue
Our words have a way of coming alive and manifesting itself
At some point it will take on shape and will become active
We are the by product of the words that we speak
Speak healthy, wholesome words into your life
Effective results will unfold right before your very eyes

WAITING FOR YOU LORD

Lord, I'm waiting for you
Waiting to get a word from you
Waiting here for you Lord
Waiting on the threshing floor
Waiting like how Ruth waited for Boaz, as she gleaned in the field
Waiting for divine instruction and divine inspiration

I'm waiting
I'm waiting Lord, for you to speak to me
I'm waiting for you to direct me
Waiting on you Lord

Waiting for divine impartation, waiting for special instruction
Waiting on you Lord, waiting to get a word from you
Your word is a ray of hope. It gets me through my darkest hour
Your word brings upliftment and gives me consolation
It points me in the right direction, when I've gotten off track

SURPRISE

You have became very dear to me, after all, you were the
Mastermind behind the scene, behind the whole drama
You both came up with the idea to secretly surprise me that night
You was the driver that drove that big white trailer, and transported him
While he hid himself in the back of the truck
Together you all cleverly organized and implemented a strategic
Plan that turned out successfully, it was pulled off beautifully
The time and designated meeting place was diligently sorted out
By you two, I remembered speaking to him earlier on the phone that day
And he asked me to meet you after I leave work, because he had
Given you something that he wanted me to pick up for him
I headed over to that particular meeting place that night
I was curious and was left in suspense

I wondered to myself what could be so urgent
For me to pick up this late hour of the night
I arrived at the place, you greeted me with a smile
He came out of no where and just jumped out of the truck
I was startled, surprised, and over joy all at the same time
This was more than your typical Cocktail Party, or Tea Party
You both were laughing, but I was in Awe
What a pleasant surprise that was

POUR IT ALL ON HIM

I wish that you could lay all of your burden down at the savior's feet
When the cares and pressures of life start to overwhelm you
And you cannot find the strength or will power to battle it out
You can confidently lay your problem at the master's feet
Allow him to fix it for you, he will undoubtedly work it out
He's the solution to all of life problems
You don't have to be burden down in sorrow and despair
When you feel like your whole world is crumbling under
Call upon him, and he'll be there in a hurry
Hang in there, he'll come through for you
Keep hope alive, don't throw in the towel
Give him a chance to move the mountain for you
He'll be right there to weather your storm
Your night will disappear, and joy will come in the morning
He'll be there to guide you
He'll be there to comfort you
With words of reassurance and affirmation

LOCKED AWAY WITH YOU

You and me
Alone, in our own private world
No distractions, no interruption
No cell phone ringing, No knocking at the door
Just enjoying ourselves
In our own little love nest
Being engulfed by our
Love for each other
The only sound we hear
Is that of the love birds
As they chirped over our heads in unison
This is their way of showing
Their stamp of approval
Where have you been all my life?
How come we didn't cross path?
In the interim of life
But here we are destined together forever

YOU'RE GOOD NOURISHMENT FOR ME

You are a good source of nourishment for
My mind, my soul, body and spirit
You are good for my appetite
Thoughts of you, enhances my nutritional intake and value
Reminiscing about you and the wonderful and
Special things that we've deposited into each other's life
Only speed up my metabolism and enhances my growth
I thrive on all the positive and wholesome things
That you've brought to our relationship
I may not be able to run fast like
Usain Bolt, the fastest man in the entire world
But, whenever I see you coming
The joy I experience in seeing you
Gives me a gold medalist determination and mentality
It makes me feel like running a marathon
And I am running it with the intention to win
You are a great inspirational source
You are my love, my friend, my mentor

WHY ME

You asked the question why me?
My question to you is why not you?
Everyone on the earth have gifts, talents and abilities
Some people use it, others ignore it
You can become whatever you desire to be in life
There's an old infomercial that says Be all that you can Be
You have the potential to chase your dreams
And turn them into a reality, one dream at a time
We have certain Gifts, Talents, and abilities
That's embedded deep inside of us
Sometimes they lie dormant for years
It's up to you to allow these special
Hidden talents and gifts to become a reality

THE MAN THAT I ADMIRE

Since I've known you, I've watched you give of yourself
Repeatedly and relentlessly time and time again
You're always giving assistance to anyone
Who enter your path
I've watched you give bountifully and willingly
Never expecting anything in return
Maintaining a good attitude and always in good spirits
I want to Thank You for your endless and ongoing acts of kindness
Thank you for your commendable honesty and integrity
You are truly one of a kind
You never grew weary, got tired, grumbled or complained
You never grew weary of helping others
I've watched you draw up and cleverly executed
A plan to resolve conflicts, hard situations and issues that you faced
On so many levels, you did not break, but resourcefully, intelligently,
confidently and skillfully handled the problem
Sometimes when I think about you, I envision a craftsman
Sitting at his bench, skillfully working with his hands. I wonder how
you managed to be so multitask and diverse at the same time. I place
you on a pedestal, because you belong there. You are more valuable
than rubies, diamonds and pearls. You're a man of exemplary character
and I love you

FREEDOM OF THE MIND

Let me build up my defenses and fight back
Because they're trying to break me down
Don't hold me back, don't try to hold me captive
Don't try to place a mental block
Let me regroup and come back stronger

Go away from me, because you cannot hold me captive
You cannot take my mind
You cannot take away my God given potential
You can't take my mind, because it's my deliverance
You cannot touch my thinking, because I'm so deeply ingrafted
You can't keep me in a box, to keep me from progressing
Remove the walls of partition, tear it down
Don't try to enslave my mind
I'm breaking loose out of here
Release my shirt, let me free my mind
From this thing called mental slavery

A WONDERFUL SISTER

My lovely sister, you give off a sweet aroma
Your countenance is so radiant, that's why you are my eldest sister
You are an excellent role model and lead by example
During my adolescence years, you nurtured and lead me
On the right path, you did not spoil me
You treated me like an adult, and that's why
I became responsible at a very young age
When I was a teenager, I use to walk around
With a small brown paper bag
I use to place my coins, my keys inside of that little bag
I remember one day in particular, my sister said to me
Why don't you just get a purse, that way you can
Place everything inside of it, and it would look way better
I chuckled because I found it to be amusing
I remember all the good times that we shared
Thank you for guiding me throughout my adolescent years

PRINCE CHARMING

My Nephews, I am elated and honored to be acquainted
With you all, such wonderful and handsome young men
I've watched you all grow up from a tot
And have developed into responsible people in society
And law abiding citizens of this country
I especially love the bond that you all share
I love your mannerism and fine etiquette
You all are so shy, diverse, and unique in all your own way
You all are so different and creative too
To my Nephew, the one with that beautiful artistic ability
You know who you are
I am fond of your incredible work of art
Keep up the good work, and continue to deliver your artistry
Continue to draw and continue to use your skills and imagination

THE SKY IS THE LIMIT

You have value, you have worth
Never under estimate the power that lies within you
Because you are greater and mightier than you think
Our minds, our intellect possesses great and mighty things
Feed your mind with healthy thoughts and meditation
Learn to be mentally creative
Speak to your destiny, tell it that you are in charge

Begin to believe that you can achieve anything that
You perceive, no matter how insignificant you may think it is
Never put any limitations on the things that you can do
You can do anything in life, once you put your mind to it
Learn to activate and unleash the greatness that's inside
Of you, you'll be happy that you did

THANKSGIVING

I want to thank you Lord for all that you have done for me
Thank you for all the many blessings that you've bestow upon me
I want to give you thanks without asking you for anything
Just for the fact that I am existing is more than
Enough to give you thanks for
Thank you for daily blessings and provision
And for supplying my daily need
Calling upon you and knowing that you are there
Listening attentively, ready to respond, ready to give a helping hand
It's so soothing and so refreshing
It's like drinking a fresh cool glass of water
You quench my thirst, and bring me total satisfaction
Help me not to worry about the things that I don't have
Help me to be satisfy with the things that I do have
Without you my life would be incomplete mode

BIG BROTHER

Brother, you are unique and talented in your own way
Full of passion and full of life
I compliment you for being the man that you have become today
You are truly a provider in every sense of the word
You work long and hard hours to ensure that
Your family have the necessary amenities needed in life
To live a comfortable and satisfying life
You are electrically inclined and continue to use
That God given ability all the time
I remember when we were growing up
You used to bring home all sorts of old
Electrical appliances and fixtures that you found on the street
You would pull them apart and fixed them
I remembered that old microwave that you brought home one day
You managed to fix it and got it to work again
It's amazing how your boys developed the same skills and abilities
Thanks for the sacrifices that you've made throughout the years

TURN IT AROUND

I hope that we could all learn not to avenge our enemies
I wish that we can learn to do good to those, who don't treat us right
I know that this will not be an easy task, and is not an easy step
It's not easy to forget the past hurts, and pain they've afflicted upon us
It's hard to forget about all the wrongs that they have done
Especially when we've been wounded by family, familiar and close friends
Some of us are left with scars and embedded wounds buried
Deep down inside carrying around for years upon years
But we must try to exhale all the pain, past hurts, animosity, bitterness
Resentment, anger, hatred and the tension that has build up
Don't harbor it in your heart, get rid of it, let it go, don't resist
If our enemies are hungry let's feed them, if they are thirsty give them drink
Some of us have been talked about, ridicule, mistreated
Used, abused, mistreated, ostracized, handled incorrectly
Never mind, don't worry about it, because they are
Truly the one who will have to deal with the
Consequences when it comes, just release yourself
Allow the healing process to take place and turn it around, let the recovery process begin, take a step into a new avenue, develop positive reinforcements
Only then you'll realize that the benefits will outweigh the effort

43

YOU HAVE THE KEY
TO MY HEART

You're the marksman of love, you headed straight for
The heart and never missed when you hit
You captivated mind, soul, body and spirit
You targeted the very core of my being
You've enriched and deposited a lot of love
And positive things into my life
I'm making a proclamation and is making
My voice heard
I love and treasure the memories that we shared together
I've found a real gem, a precious stone
You deserve the man of the year award
You got the key to unlock my heart
You got the password to enter my heart
And you got that password lock

THE MEANING OF LOVE

I love you unconditionally, not only for today
But for a lifetime. I'm moved by every little detail about you
The way you walk and the way you talk
You're the one that I hoped for
Heaven must have sent you, you're the one that I dreamed of
You're the man of my dreams

Your love has held me captive
I'm bound endlessly by your love
Oh no, I cannot get away
I'm entrapped by your venom
And is now a victim of your love

You gave me something to write about
You gave me something to smile about
You gave me something to think about
I'm connected to you like a magnet
I'm drawn into your world in ways you'll never imagine

HAVE YOUR WAY IN ME

Make your home right here Lord
Take up residence in me
Come on in
Take off your shoes off and make yourself comfortable
Father God, because I'm making room for you to do your thing in me
To accomplish your goal through me

Have your way in me
Have your way in me
Have your way in me
Dear Lord

You've been knocking at my door for a long time
Trying to enter, but access was denied
You kept knocking and didn't give up on me
The door is now open, come on in and have your way in me
Fulfill your desire in me Lord

Have your way in me
You've been waiting patiently to enter my world
I now give you complete access to my world, You've entered the threshold
Have your way in me, Let your desire unfold land manifest in me

YOU BRING ME JOY

Boobee, I shed a tear because of the happiness and joy
That you've brought into my life
Life is uncertain, but one thing I'm certain about
And is that I love you now and for eternity
Just want to maximize each moment spend with you
Being with you makes the world a beautiful place to live
Your love has captured me, and held me captive
You have defined my life in more ways than one
I'm devoted to our love because it's a special kind of love
More than the kind found in story books
More than Romeo and Juliet
I love you endlessly, and is devoted to our love
What I feel for you
I continue to bring out in my songs
You were the missing puzzle that completes me
So glad you're in my life
Loving you endlessly
And sincerely

BE A WELL WISHER

I've always wondered to myself, why some people don't
Want to see others be successful in life
I don't know what their motive or their logic is behind it
Whatever the reason is, I believe that it's selfish and self centered
I've often seen this behavior displayed repeatedly
And always asked the question why do
People behave in this manner
I've said to myself, If they learned to place their energy
And attention on good deeds and positivity
Then maybe their miserable world would turn around
They will progress, and their life will become a success
They desperately try to ruin
What someone else is trying so hard to achieve
Why can't they wish people the very best
Why can't they wish them joy, success, peace and happiness
What they sow, is what they'll reap
If they learn to be a well wisher
Then I believe that their lives will become prosperous
If they learn to invest and deposit good
Things into people's lives
Then without a doubt, they'll have
A wholesome and healthy tomorrow

YOU'RE MY REFUGE

You're my refuge, my hiding place, my peace of mind

My sanctuary, Lord, you're my Solace

You're my rock on which I stand

You're my comforter, when I need comfort

Lord, you're my strength when I'm weak

You're my shelter in the time of storm

You're the Alpha and Omega

The beginning and the end

You're above all kings and kingdoms, principalities, powers

You rule supreme in the heavens

You rule supreme on the earth, your kingdom reigns forever
and ever

You're my doctor when I'm sick, my Jehovah jirah, my
provider, you're the mighty counselor, my prince of peace Lord,
you've been my navigator, stirred me in the right path

And right direction

When I was lost and couldn't find my way

IT WAS FOR ME AND FOR YOU

The shame and humility that Jesus bore that day

As he hung on that old rugged cross, he cried out in agony. . . it's finished, as he freely laid down his life

It was for you and me. . . that our savior died

He bear the excruciating crown of thorns that they placed on his head, and drank the bitter cup of vinegar

That they gave him when he cried out for thirst

It was all on the behalf of you and me, it was all done for you and for me

He could of freed himself that day by calling thousands of angels, to set him free from his pain and agony

But he had to fulfill the master's plan

He had to fulfill the mater's plan

He had to fulfill the master's plan

"REAL LOVE"

The love we feel for each other is more powerful than
Any two antioxidant combined together
Sincerity, honesty, integrity
Is the by produce of our relationship
Trust, Respect, Commitment, Loyalty
Is the building block on
Which our relationship stands
I love you, You love me
Together we'll reach our destiny
Did I tell you that I love you lately?
I love you twenty four seven
Twice on weekends
And triple on holidays
Your love has left an indelible mark
Oh my heart that will never be erased
There's no turning back now
Our love is for Eternity

RIDING ON HIS ETERNAL WINGS

He holds me so gently in the palm of his dear hands

There I'm covered, I'm covered in his precious blood

And all through life's journey, he guides me safely o'er

He eliminates all of the darkness and overrides every storm

I'm riding, just riding under his eternal wings. Under his wings, there's no turbulence, no pitfall or danger zone

In his loving arms, I feel so safe, so safe and secure

I'm riding, just riding under his eternal wings

Under his wings, I'm safely abiding

There my burdens, my burdens are lifted

And all shackles are broken off

There I'm protected and is free from all harm

I don't have to worry and there's no reason for alarm

MY CLOSEST FRIEND

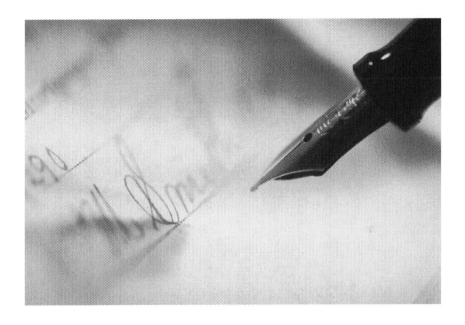

My Pen and my Paper have become my closest friend
I've learned to depend on them when I want to brainstorm
Or just to simply jot things down
They've encouraged me to be creative with my thoughts
When I want to express my inner feelings and emotions
I pour it out on them, and they've received me with opened arms
My pen and my paper don't place any limitations or conditions
On what I can write or say
I've relied on them when I want to exhale. My Pen and my Paper,
You've allowed me to express my deepest and intimate thoughts
You've embraced me and allow me to flow like a ready writer
My pen and my paper has allowed me to express myself

You have inspired me, and have erased every doubt
With you, I can flow with confidence and without reservation
You've invited me in, and opened up my thinking ability
You're my valuable instrument, you release me and gave me a piece of mind
You're my compass, my GPS, you propelled me
You've navigated my thoughts and showed them where to go
You listened to me, and have allowed my mind
And Imagination to run wild
You mean the world to me

OUR SAVIOR PRAYED

He went all alone in the garden
As his custom was, away from the disciples
Away from the mixed multitude
There he knelt on his knees and interceded
Till his sweat, till his sweat became like drops of blood

Oh. . . it was for you and for me, that our savior humbly prayed
He knelt in total submission as he prayed for our sins
He completely surrendered, as he bowed down on his knees
Oh in that solitary place called the garden of Gethsemane
He cried out on our behalf as, he send up the petition
If that isn't love, then I don't know what else is.

No one else, no one else, could ever duplicate this act of love
Because it was all laid out in the master plan
He took all, he took all of our burden
And laid them at the feet of, at the feet of, feet of the cross

WITHOUT YOU

I've been waiting patiently by the phone for you to call
Waiting minute by minute, hour by hour
Until the momentum was right, I don't ever want you out of my sight
Cause you've filled my life with joy and satisfaction

Without you my life, my world would turn upside down
Without you my blue sky would turn into gray
Without you my day would turn into midnight
Without you my life would be in absolute turmoil

I have an insatiable appetite for you baby
I desire more and more of you, time and time again
I carry you in my heart throughout the day, and throughout the night
I hope you feel the teardrops
When they fall from my heart
I'm crying out for your love

EXHALE, BE IN CONTROL

I believe that malice, anger, bitterness and jealousy didn't develop
Overnight, but over a period of time
It starts out small and with time, tension builds up
Then it begins to manifest outwardly
Many people today are struggling with this behavior
On a day to day basis, If not dealt with, erased or become obsolete
It will develop into a bigger problem
I believe that the solution to resolving this problem
Is self awareness, be willing to see the problem, admit it
Find out what's causing it, target the problem head on
Make a list of triggers, find out how
These feelings developed in the first place
It's important to identify your own problem
So you'll be able to manage your own behavior
Consider how it hurt or upset you, and how it affect others
Be willing to talk about it, talk about emotional things that hurts you
Include all the little details, no matter how minute it may seem
Talk to a friend about it, seek counseling if necessary
Get the help that you need, be open and honest about it
The objective is to release those feelings and to get the problem resolved
Take back your life, take control, develop a healthy mental attitude
Take a brave step in maintaining a healthier lifestyle

THANK YOU MOTHER

Mother, you shaped and enriched our lives in so many ways
I have so many good things to say about you. I commend you for
The fine job you did in raising us
You instilled good morals, good mannerism, proper etiquette
Those values molded us into the adults that we are today
Thank you for nurturing and taking care of us during our young and
tender years
You left us in the care of our dear grandmother, as you migrated
To the United States, in search for a better life and to find greener pasture
You worked long and hard hours in the cold, to make the ends meet
You never forsake or neglected us. You always made sure that grandmother
And grandfather had monetary funds to sustain us
We never went to bed hungry
We had plenty to eat, and plenty to share
You deserve a mother of the year award, and a standing ovation
Thanks for the relentless sacrifices that you made for us throughout
the years

PRECIOUS LITTLE ONES,
SO HANDLE WITH CARE

Children are the heritage of the Lord
They are precious in his sight
Children are innocent and they replicate what
They're exposed to in their world
Be careful what you're teaching and exposing them to
Children are sharp, smart, they are quick learners
They are equipped and are vulnerable
They learn and adapt quickly to this ever-changing environment
They are more open and are easily influenced
By what's around them, whether that be good or bad
Instill good sound values in them
Train them up in the right and proper way
Train them up in the ways of the Lord, so
That they have a firm foundation on which to stand
Careful of what you're imparting unto them
As you mold them throughout
Their tender years, because they are tomorrows future

POSITIVE REINFORCEMENT

Don't be sad, but be happy with joy and elation
Rise with the morning sun, start your day with
Strength and renewed vigor
Don't allow the clouds to hang low over your head
To keep your spirit low, perk yourself up
Rise to the occasion, spring up like a jack in the box
Don't stay down drowning yourself in emotion and deep sorrow
I know that it is not going to be easy
It is easier to say than to actual do
But we got to start somewhere
We can start with changing our mind set
By rearranging our outlook on life
We can mentally conquer and change our thinking
We can change our present circumstances
And don't have to settle for defeat
We have the power to rearrange our focus
And to change our course of direction

THE INTENSITY OF MY HEART

Can you handle the passion
Can you handle the thrill
Can you handle the intensity of the heartfelt messages
Coming from out of my heart
Do you need a love doctor, to give you sound advice
To help you through the day
And to help you through the night
Cause the fire is intensifying, the flame is getting high

    Telling you that I love you
    Is barely scratching the surface
    What I feel you for is beyond human comprehension

We got the recipe for love
I love you, and you love me
And together we'll reach new horizons
Beyond our wildest dream
With you in my life, the sun is always shinning
Even when it's windy outside, your love keeps me warm

LEARN TO LET IT GO

Don't be a hater, Don't allow bad memories, and bad experiences
Of the past to hold you hostage and cause you from moving forward
Why are you so bitter with the world
Learn to exhale all those negative feelings
Exhale, Let it Out it's no good for your health
No good for your mind, soul, body and spirit
Don't resist that little voice inside of you telling you to Let it Go
Why are you still harboring and holding on to
Past hurts, pains, failures and disappointments
Learn to release people out of your heart
Don't allow the wounds to flare up and
Fester like a bad sore
Take the bandage off, allow the healing
Process to begin, get the load off
Learn to forgive, and to embrace people
No one said it would be easy, but you have to start somewhere
Shake the excess weight off, and inhale positivity

A VALUABLE LESSON LEARNED

Get the facts first, before you draw any conclusions
Don't thrive on speculations and mere "hear says"
Be wise. Do your homework
Gather all the proof. And evidence you may need. Search diligently
Get all the facts and details before you prejudge
Or past judgment. Think it through
Passing judgment nullifies the uniqueness and
And individuality of others
Gather all the facts and important data
Put all bias aside
Don't be anxious. Relax
The old saying goes the proof is in the pudding
Don't be hasty, don't be in a hurry
Don't be quick to point the finger
You may ruin someone's credibility, life or integrity

YOU DON'T HAVE
TO LIVE IN DESPAIR

Don't live in despair and hopelessness. Be strong
Don't stay down, rise up, stand up, stay in the race and fight for your life
You may feel like you're at the end of your rope
You may feel lonely, and like you're at your wit's end
If this is you, hold on, don't give up
Don't yield to oppression and negative feelings
Don't succumb to doubt and fear, it's a terrible disease
You may feel like your world is sinking fast
You do have a lively hope, so pull yourself out
Come out of the rubble, shake off the excess dust

You don't have to listen to doubt, you don't have
To listen to those negative thoughts
Readjust your focus, realign your thoughts, and fight back
Think positive happy thoughts, get a grip
Learn to overcome your fears, relax, unwind
Liberate yourself from the enemy called fear, doubt and loneliness
Build up your defenses and fight back, don't look behind you
Call on the Lord he will help you, what are you waiting for
He's standing right there to set you free
Lift yourself out of the rubble and get back on track

NEVER GIVE UP

One more day in life's mystical journey
I'm standing firm and never giving up
Hurdle after hurdle, battle after battle
Triumph after triumph, victory after victory
I'm never putting down the baton
But will stay in the race
Many times I've gotten weak, and my feet buckled under
The clouds and atmospheric turbulences
Sometimes got rough, but I'm keeping goal driven
Because I have a dream, and an aim in view
Thanks to the ones, who didn't stand
With me or support me
You only accelerated me into my God given potential
And pushed me further into my destiny
The more you talked about me
Is the more God elevated me
You can never keep a good woman down